# HOW
# POOP
# CAN SAVE THE
# WORLD

**"If you're a human and you're not sure what poop can do for you—read this book!"**
— *The National Poo Museum, UK*

Published in 2022 by Welbeck Children's Books Limited
An Imprint of the Welbeck Publishing Group
Based in London and Sydney.
www.welbeckpublishing.com

Text copyright © 2022 John Townsend
Illustration copyright © 2022 Welbeck Publishing Limited

Designer: Andrew Thomas/Forge Design
Design Manager: Matt Drew
Editor: Jenni Lazell
Production: Melanie Robertson

ISBN: 978 1 78312 852 5

Printed in the UK
10 9 8 7 6 5 4 3 2 1

FSC
www.fsc.org
MIX
Paper from
responsible sources
FSC® C171272

# HOW POOP CAN SAVE THE WORLD

WELBECK

John Townsend          Illustrated by Steve Brown

# CONTENTS

# INTRODUCTION

Everyone poops. They've always done it. But now there's more of it than ever.

Yikes—will poop destroy our planet? Will it take over the world? Will we all sink into poopy oblivion?

So much for the nightmare—now for the good news. Poop power could actually **SAVE THE WORLD!**

# A heap of steaming questions!

All living creatures need food and water for energy and to grow. But they all need to get rid of waste once that food and water has been used. That's a lot of waste—there's non-stop poop production happening all around our planet. In fact, there are more people pooping today than at any time in the world's history. So is the world about to be totally pooped?

 **Where does all that waste go?**

 **Is it all dangerous?**

 **How can we use it to help save the planet?**

You will be amazed by some of the answers coming up in these pages from the stunning science of **POOP POWER**. Get ready for a big dollop of surprises.

**WARNING!** Some adults might turn up their noses at you reading this book!

CHAPTER 1

# POOP BASICS
## THE BOTTOM LINE

What exactly is poop and why
can it be so amazing?

Basically, poop is just the waste material left over
from our digestive system. Scientists call our
solid waste "feces, excrement, or stools." But they
probably just call it poop in private.

## Down to basics

Poop is made of dead cells from inside our gut, lots of **bacteria**, **water**, and **plant fibers** from food that didn't get fully digested in the stomach. The color, shape, and smell of poop is affected by what we eat. Our diet can also affect whether poop floats or sinks in water.

### DID YOU KNOW?

**Poop should be disposed of safely as it can spread many diseases. Funnily enough, even scientists didn't always know that. In the last 150 years they have been working like stink to understand all those tiny micro-organisms living inside poop.**

# Bodily waste

It only takes seconds for your chewed-up food to reach your stomach, where it becomes a sloppy, churning liquid. As it gets pushed on through your intestines, the nutrients are absorbed into your bloodstream. It takes about 12 hours to digest a meal completely. The leftover sludge and waste get squeezed out through the large intestine and then from the body. Each day about 2.5 gallons of mashed up food and liquid go through your body but only a small amount ends up as solid poop.

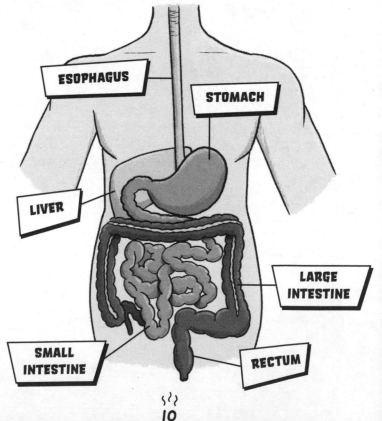

ESOPHAGUS

STOMACH

LIVER

LARGE INTESTINE

SMALL INTESTINE

RECTUM

## For the record:

The average adult poops about 14 ounces each day (like four big lemons' worth)

That's something like 320 pounds of poop every year (about the size of a giant panda—or a very giant lemon!)

The poop produced by all humans on Earth in one year is about 660 billion pounds—that's something like 60 Great Pyramids of Giza (or 3,000 billion lemons).

Add the mountains of poop from all the animals on Earth and you can begin to see how big this subject can be. So, let's step into the vast world of poop—but be careful where you tread!

# In the beginning there was poop...

For thousands of years, poop has been very useful stuff. True, it's often nasty, messy, smelly, and even harmful. But when put to good use, poop can be a valuable material. When it rots down into rich crumbly manure, it's great for the soil. People have been spreading human and animal poop on the land and growing tasty crops from it for centuries. Manure adds important nutrients, such as nitrogen, to the soil, which helps plants to grow really well.

## Useful poop-pulp

As well as making great garden compost, animal manure was used long ago to make paper. In Africa and Asia, elephant dung packed with plant fibers was made into pulp, pressed and dried to make parchment. Other animals, such as horses, llamas, and kangaroos, have also made useful deposits for paper makers. Maybe paper should be called pooper! On average, one lump of elephant poop can make 25 sheets of large paper. Panda poop in China is even made into—guess what? Toilet tissue!

## Poop with sparkle

Scientists who study human sewage (yes, some start their careers at the very BOTTOM) have found all sorts of ingredients in poop, including gold and silver. Tiny particles of valuable minerals and metals from different products end up inside our bodies. When these come out in poop and are flushed down the toilet, they end up in sewage treatment plants. A study of sewage found that poop from one million Americans could contain as much as $11.8 million worth of gold. We could all be sitting on a goldmine!

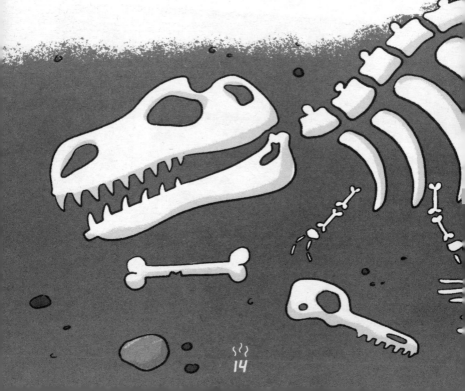

# DID YOU KNOW?

Poop has been around for millions of years. Dinosaurs left behind huge dollops of it. Just imagine the size of some of their monster poops! Lumps of their fossil poop are found today in many places. These solid remains, called coprolite, can be polished and worn as jewelry. Would you wear coprolite in your hair? No need then for shamPOO!

## The danger of poop

If you never think twice about popping into the bathroom for a number two, you are lucky. After all, millions of people don't have the luxury of a proper toilet. 4.5 billion people around the world don't have toilets that safely flush away their waste. That means millions of tons of human waste go untreated, with more than 90 percent of sewage in many parts of the world going straight into streams, lakes, and rivers. And that's where many people collect their water to drink.

At least 1.8 billion people worldwide drink water that has germs in it from poop. Children especially can become very sick from drinking it. About 842,000 people are thought to die every year from drinking water with poop in it. That's just one more reason why getting to grips with poop is so important for the future of our planet.

DANGER!
NOT SAFE TO DRINK

Tank with hungry worms inside

## Poo-lution solution

A big problem in many remote villages of
the world is the total lack of sanitation.
Running water and flushing toilets are
expensive and need plumbers to keep things
working. One answer is the "Tiger Toilet" which
needs no water—just a container full of tiger worms
that love munching on poop. Within six months
these worms turn human waste into very
useful, non-smelly compost. Yum.

## How does a Tiger Toilet work?

Instead of poop plopping into a bowl of water, it falls
into a compartment full of tiger worms. In nature,
tiger worms survive on the droppings of animals like
cattle and horses. So, they are just as happy in a Tiger
Toilet as they would be wriggling around in the soil.
The worms don't try to escape because they are busy
enjoying turning human waste into compost, making it
just right for spreading on growing crops. And yes, even
if a tiger uses a Tiger Toilet, the worms will still do their
job and turn its poop into user-friendly fertilizer.

# Random animal poop facts

 Ancient Romans used to dye their hair blond with pigeon poop.

 For nearly 40 years, until 2009, a Moose Dropping Festival was held in Alaska. This included a Moose Dropping Game, where numbered nuggets of moose droppings were dropped from a helicopter and people placed bets on where they would land. Hopefully not on the chocolate chip cookies!

IS THIS AMOOOSING TO YOU?

During the American Civil War, bat poop full of potassium was used to make gunpowder. The power of bat poop (called guano) can be explosive!

 The bare-nosed wombat is a furry Australian marsupial that squeezes out nearly 100 six-sided poops every day—the size and shape of sugar cubes. That's quite a party trick. As many an Australian might say, "The squarer the poop, the healthier the wombat."

**Your verdict so far ... POOP–friend, foe, or superhero?**

CHAPTER 2

# POOP THROUGH HISTORY

## THE WHIFF OF CHANGE

For centuries people have used poop for fuel and for building materials. Burning dried dung or plastering it over walls kept people warm and it still does. In many countries cow dung is mixed with clay for plastering walls. Chemicals in fresh dung react with minerals in clay to help harden the mixture and prevent cracking—and it's soon stink-free!

Early European settlers on the Great Plains of the United States also used dried buffalo dung as a fuel. They called it buffalo chips.

## Ancient poop power

Dried animal dung was used as fuel to burn on fires in ancient Egypt and Persia. Cow or buffalo dung has long been used as fuel in India, too. "Dung cakes," made by hand and then dried, burn well, especially for heating cooking pots. Not only do dung cakes make cheap and effective fuel, they also get rid of smelly waste that would otherwise attract flies.

## Streets of dung

For five thousand years until the development of steam engines in the early 1800s, the only way to travel on land faster than walking was by horse. Horses were everywhere. Towns and cities were full of them. That meant piles of horse dung everywhere, too. By 1800, busy cities like New York had a serious horse poop problem.

## Phew!

In hot summers, horse dung dried on city streets and the dust blew everywhere. In winter, streets became a sloppy stinking mess. Manure attracted millions of flies that carried killer diseases like typhoid. Many streets were piled so high with dung that paths had to be dug for women in long dresses to walk through. Children with brooms worked as "crossing sweepers" on street corners, hoping to get paid by people trying to make their way across. Some children earned money by collecting dog poop and selling it to leather tanneries. A bubbling vat of poop apparently softens leather beautifully. Let's take their word for it!

# The power of poop to kill

A killer disease spread by poop is cholera. From 1831-1866, at least 40,000 people died from cholera in London, UK. People didn't know the disease spread in sewage and that cholera bacteria got into drinking water. They thought disease spread in smelly air.

In the 1840s richer people began to have flushing toilets connected to drains. The quick removal of poop from their homes was meant to prevent smelly air spreading cholera around the city. Oops—big mistake. Suddenly, huge amounts of sewage were being flushed into the river. We now know cholera is spread in poopy river water.

## Big risk

Yet another cholera epidemic struck London in 1854 when sewage seeped into a well. Over 600 people died after drinking from that one well. A doctor named John Snow was sure cholera spread in dirty water rather than in smelly air. He insisted on cleaning up rivers and water supplies. Sadly, he died before other scientists began to understand the bacteria in human waste. It took the Great Stink of 1858 to make everyone think about the power of poop and health.

## The Great Stink

By the summer of 1858, the smell from the River Thames was so bad, people called it "The Great Stink." Just one drop of Thames water, full of foul germs, was all it took to kill—sometimes in hours. Anyone unlucky enough to fall into the river wouldn't stand a chance.

As the summer got hotter in 1858, the river level dropped, dumping layers of human poop many feet deep on the muddy banks. Queen Victoria had to cancel a boat trip on the Thames because of the smell. She was not amused ... Politicians in the Parliament buildings even had the curtains soaked in bleach to help keep the smell away. Things got so bad, they had to do something drastic. It was time to bring in the poop engineers ...

The engineer, Joseph Bazalgette, designed and built over 80 miles of large main sewers, 1,100 miles of street sewers, four pumping stations, two treatment works, and three embankments to solve the poop problem.

## Cleaning up Paris

Like London, Paris owes its sewer system to epidemics of deadly diseases in the 19th century. Then, bedpans and buckets were emptied from windows into streets and flowed into rivers along with horse manure—to end up in drinking water. In 1832, people began suffering from fever, chest pains, and vomiting. Most died within a day or two. Within two weeks, 7,000 people were dead, which grew to 19,000 in six months. Something had to be done to stop cholera spreading through the streets.

By 1878, Paris had built an underground sewage system 375 miles long and gutters were moved to the sides of streets. Tourists even came to the city to tour the new sewers. For a city famous for its perfumes, L'eau de Caca (Poop water) was no longer available! With the arrival of cars, horse manure began to reduce. But then exhaust waste from engines became deadly. It's just as well poop is making a comeback—this time to fuel cleaner vehicles and make cities far safer. More about that in Chapter 6.

# A quick history of the toilet

 In Ancient Egypt, only the wealthy had indoor stone toilets. Poorer people made do with a wooden stool with a hole in it. Both had a pit underneath, with sand to collect the waste. Then someone would have to empty it somewhere out of the way.

 Around 800 BCE, the Romans built sewers as well as public lavatories lined with benches of toilets. Sometimes a group of Romans would sit on these benches in a line and discuss business (no, not that sort) while relieving themselves. Then it was a matter of "pass the sponge on a stick" for a quick wipe—and back to gladiator games.

 Many medieval castles had a small privy called a garderobe that jutted out over a moat. Just think what plopped down into the water below. Who would want to invade a castle when fired at from a garderobe?

Before the invention of the flushing toilet, many ordinary homes kept a chamber pot tucked away. Someone then had to empty it—often out of the window into the street. You can imagine the rest.

 A godson of Queen Elizabeth I (1533-1603) named Sir John Harrington invented the first flushing toilet. In 1592, Queen Elizabeth visited his house and was so impressed, she ordered one for herself —maybe for her own special throne room.

 The Victorian inventor Thomas Crapper adapted the design of flushing toilets and sold hundreds around London with his name on them. When American soldiers posted to the UK saw the name "crapper," they took the term back to the States and used it—you can probably guess how.

 By the late 1800s, many workers' homes in towns were built with outside toilets—often at the end of a yard and shared with many other large families. Queueing in the rain to poop was all part of the fun!

A big problem through history has been how to get rid of poop from homes, streets, and rivers. Where does it end up and what happens to it? Prepare to be stunned ...

CHAPTER 3

# POOP ON THE MOVE

## FLUSHED WITH SUCCESS

Removing poop so it's quickly out of sight (and smell) has always been a challenge. Believe it or not, people have always worked in the "poop disposal industry." You could say it's big business full of . . . opportunities. After all, an old saying goes "where there's muck there's money."

## Night-men

Poop has made some people stinking rich. That was even so in Tudor times. At the time of King Henry VIII (1491-1547), many people would "relieve themselves" in shared spaces—pooping into a cesspit. In time, cesspits would get full and overflow. That's when "gong farmers," or night-men, would come in at night to take away piles of poop, also known as night soil.

To make sure they collected all the foul sludge, gong farmers would get right in the cesspit with their shovels, sometimes up to their waist in waste. Often children did this job then loaded up carts to dump everything on the edge of town for spreading on the land. Then it was back home to sleep in the same clothes—with no possibility of a bath. It was just a matter of taking their work home and sleeping on it!

## Who flung dung?

Although using poop as a weapon might not save the world, it may have won a few battles through history.

In 12th century China, a large type of poop catapult fired a nasty mix at the enemy. A "bomb" filled with human poop, gunpowder, and poison was lit with a hot poker and flung. Anyone hit by that would probably surrender immediately and go home for a bath!

Even in more recent history, in 2009, a Russian inventor designed a "poop cannon." When soldiers inside a tank needed to poop, they would do so into a special type of shell casing with enough room inside for poop and explosives. They would then load the shell into the tank's gun and fire it at the enemy. Please don't try this at home.

## Poop in motion—where does it go today?

Modern towns and cities have vast networks of sewer pipes running under them that swish rivers of poop and dirty water far away—we hope. Along with all the water from our sinks, showers, and streets, toilet waste, called effluent, gushes through the sewage system all the way to a treatment plant. Here everything sloshes into massive tanks where it slowly settles.

## A major motion picture ...

All the solids sink to the bottom and the water at the top
of the tank is skimmed off to be treated. Layers of poop
build up in the sludge that's left behind. Next comes the
smart part. The smelly sludge is stirred up so that the
billions of micro-organisms inside the poop can breathe
in oxygen and get extra active. They quickly munch away
on all the nasty stuff and start the big clean-up process.
Bacteria biology does much of the disposal work.

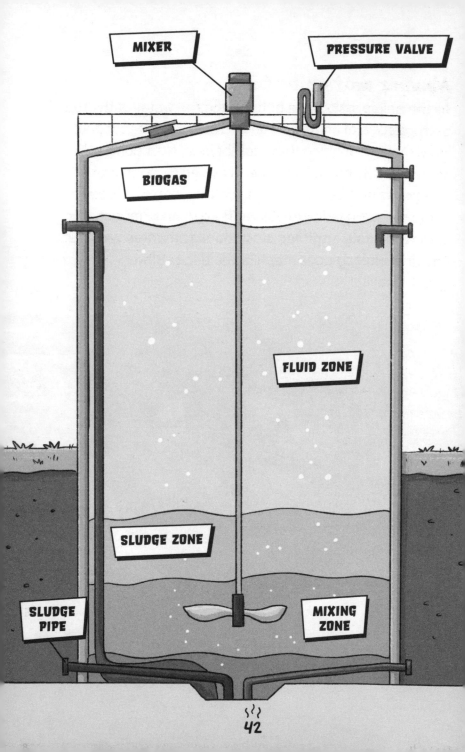

MIXER

PRESSURE VALVE

BIOGAS

FLUID ZONE

SLUDGE ZONE

SLUDGE PIPE

MIXING ZONE

42

## Moving on

In the next tank, called a digester, the sludge is heated so that special bacteria can thrive and easily break down the gloop into water and gases. Eventually the water is filtered and clean enough to drink and the gases can be used, too. But that's not all ... the remaining liquid sludge is dried out in another tank that works like a spin dryer. With all the water spun out, the dried-out disease-free sludge left behind makes great fertilizer—called biosolids. One person's poop in a year could make biosolids to fill 10 bags of sugar (but probably not as sweet). Just right for enriching the soil.

Maybe the tasty lettuce, tomatoes, or strawberries you eat owe their delicious flavor to human biosolids. Scientists insist this natural fertilizer is far better for the soil than the chemicals in artificial fertilizers. Even so, biosolids from some sewage are still sent to landfill and wasted. In the future, human poop biosolids will become even more important for farming and feeding the world.

## Animal poop on the move

If you think the deluge of human poop over Earth each day seems scary, can you dare to imagine how much animal poop is piling up every minute? Two amazing facts:

 **You don't often see much of it**

 **It keeps Earth alive, green, and thriving.**

How does that happen? Simple—it's all down to nature's little miracle workers—dung beetles. These insects and the dung they bury keep Earth in good shape. In fact, without the many species of dung beetle all around the world (apart from in Antarctica), we would be knee-deep in animal poop. These amazing beetles feed and nest in dung, and are vital for the breakdown and recycling of poop in the soil. Healthy ecosystems depend on the nutrients in dung that feed soil and plants. And that's thanks to poop-friendly beetles.

> Dung beetles may be small, but they are super-strong. A dung beetle can pull, push, and roll a ball of dung over a thousand times its own weight. That's like you dragging along six double-decker buses full of poop all by yourself.

# Dung down under

Dung beetles in Australia have worked wonders. Two hundred years ago people took thousands of horses, sheep, and cattle to Australia. All the extra poop was too much for Australia's native dung beetles that were only used to kangaroo and koala poop. Before long, farms filled with poop and flies as the beetles couldn't cope. Poop was getting out of control, so Australia imported dung beetles that specialized in cow dung. These soon cleared away the problem, enriched the soil, and improved habitats. Cow pats broke down in the earth, attracting a range of useful insects, worms, and fungi. Poop became a big friend again!

## Poop gas

Cow dung releases gas called methane. This can be harmful to our planet—as the next chapter shows. But when beetles bury, mix, and break down dung, they don't just improve soil and plants—they reduce the release of methane gas. That's good news for global warming, where poop can have a big part to play—as we're about to find out ...

Your verdict so far ... POOP–friend, foe, or superhero?

# CHAPTER 4

# POOP TO THE RESCUE

## GLOBAL WARMING DOWN THE PAN

Many scientists have been warning us that Earth is steadily heating up. This can affect the weather in various ways: it melts frozen landscapes, harms the oceans, raises sea levels, causes floods, and threatens wildlife and habitats. Yet it's up to us to do something about it because people are causing much of this global warming.

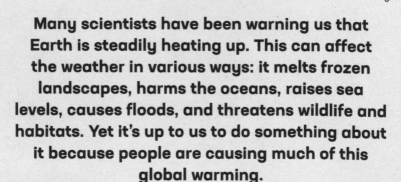

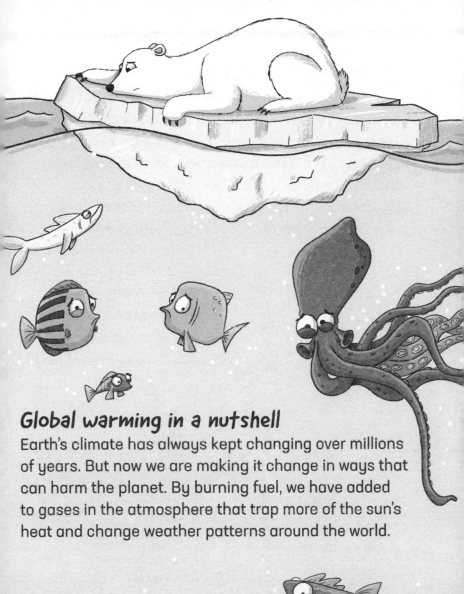

## Global warming in a nutshell

Earth's climate has always kept changing over millions of years. But now we are making it change in ways that can harm the planet. By burning fuel, we have added to gases in the atmosphere that trap more of the sun's heat and change weather patterns around the world.

# The Greenhouse Effect

Gases in the atmosphere act like a blanket around Earth that stop too much heat escaping into space. These gases, such as carbon dioxide, are vital for keeping Earth warm. But if the blanket gets thicker, everything underneath gets warmer. Scientists call the gases around the Earth "greenhouse gases" because they hold in the heat like the glass roof of a greenhouse.

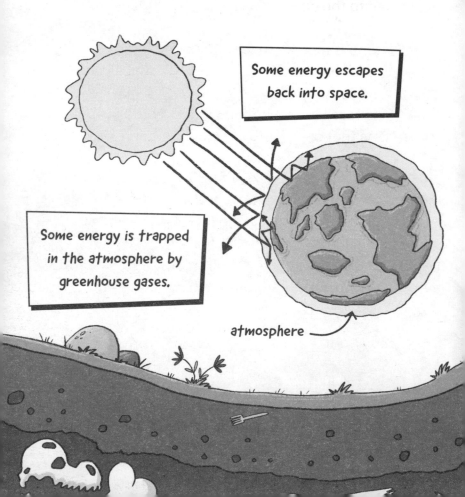

Some energy escapes back into space.

Some energy is trapped in the atmosphere by greenhouse gases.

atmosphere

## Fossil fuels and carbon—a reminder

For centuries people have burned coal, oil, and gas. These are called fossil fuels because they formed millions of years ago underground. Coal formed from buried trees, while oil and gas formed from tiny sea creatures. They all trapped carbon inside Earth. By burning such fuels, we release carbon into the air.

As gasoline is made from carbon-rich oil, vehicles release a lot of carbon gas (carbon dioxide). Even though other fuels produce some carbon dioxide, replacing fossil fuels with them will cut carbon emissions that contribute to global warming. This is where poop comes in . . .

## How does poop make useful fuel?

Back to basics ... Remember all those hungry bacteria chomping away on sewage sludge? Think of them as being so greedy that they get lots of indigestion, wind, and burps. In other words, they make gas.

The good news is, gas from poop can be burned and used for heating, cooking, or driving engines and electricity generators. Although this type of "biogas" releases some greenhouse gas, there is much less carbon dioxide than with fossil fuels. Biogas is sometimes said to be "carbon neutral."

## What does "carbon neutral" mean?

Plants absorb carbon dioxide from the atmosphere. So if an animal eats plants, its poop will contain carbon. Burning that poop or its gas will release the carbon back into the atmosphere. If this puts back carbon dioxide that was already in the atmosphere without adding any extra, this fuel is said to be carbon neutral. Unlike fossil fuel, biofuel produced cleanly shouldn't increase the overall amount of carbon dioxide on the planet.

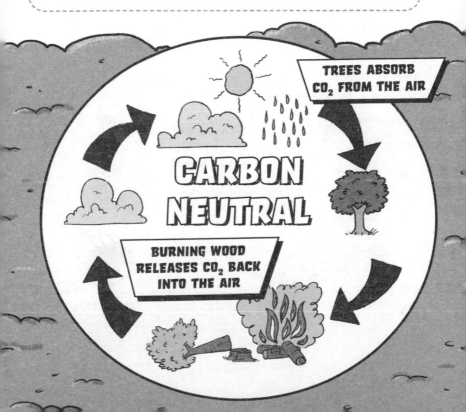

TREES ABSORB $CO_2$ FROM THE AIR

CARBON NEUTRAL

BURNING WOOD RELEASES $CO_2$ BACK INTO THE AIR

# Heating homes from poop

Sewage sludge, manure, and other waste that easily rots down (biodegradable) are stored in large, sealed tanks called biodigesters. Without oxygen inside, bacteria soon break down everything and release methane gas. This is called anaerobic digestion and all the gas is collected in pipes to be used as fuel.

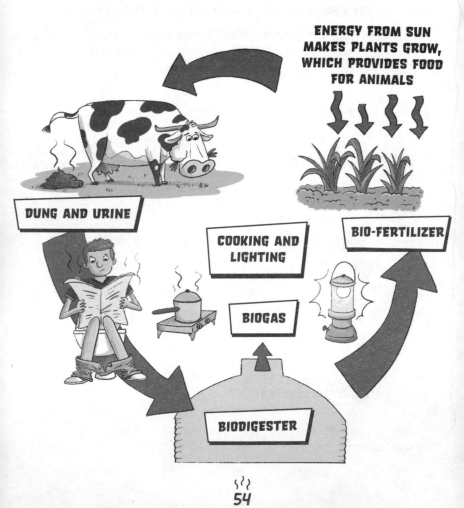

ENERGY FROM SUN MAKES PLANTS GROW, WHICH PROVIDES FOOD FOR ANIMALS

DUNG AND URINE

COOKING AND LIGHTING

BIO-FERTILIZER

BIOGAS

BIODIGESTER

**Biogas can be better for our planet than other ways of providing energy. A quick checklist:**

# CHECK LIST

☑ Biogas can generate electricity for twenty-four hours a day and for seven days a week without depending on the weather.

☑ It cuts down on our greenhouse gas emissions.

☑ It prevents a lot of waste being dumped in landfills and releasing methane gas.

☑ It can use up a lot of our sewage waste as well as other organic waste.

☑ The solid waste left over makes a rich, stink-free fertilizer.

☑ So, what's not to like?

# Gases on the rise

Ninety-nine percent of Earth's atmosphere is made up of nitrogen and oxygen gas. Two of the greenhouse gases in the remaining one percent may seem like nothing but they are very important:

## Methane

Cows burping and bogs bubbling release methane into the atmosphere—but humans make far more of this greenhouse gas by burning fossil fuels and dumping landfill waste.

## Carbon dioxide

Plants need this gas to grow and then release oxygen into the air for us and animals to breathe. By breathing out, we release carbon dioxide into the air. Burning most things releases carbon dioxide into the air.

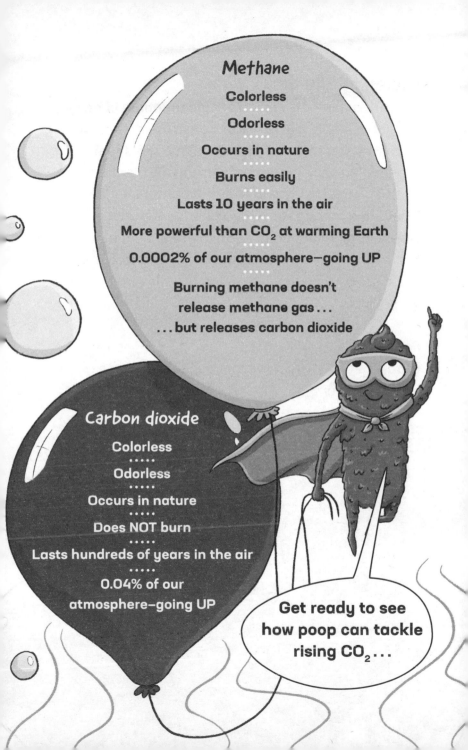

## Cleaning the air

Earth's rain forests soak up huge amounts of carbon dioxide. The trouble is, we are destroying rain forests at a worrying rate. But there is some good news. Ocean plants also suck masses of carbon dioxide from the atmosphere, and one of the things that keeps them doing this is poop. To be precise, it's the vast swirls of whale poop churning around the sea.

Microscopic phytoplankton

# Whale poop to the rescue!

Very tiny plants in the sea (marine algae called phytoplankton) produce more than half of the world's oxygen. They also feed huge numbers of sea creatures. But that's not all—they store masses of carbon, which means they are vital in cutting down the amount of $CO_2$ in the atmosphere. And what feeds this Earth-saving phytoplankton? Whale poop—a mineral-rich miracle fertilizer of the ocean! As the largest creature on the planet, a blue whale can poop over 50 gallons in one go, so there's a lot of it about... and it's doing wonders for our planet!

## What if?

Just think how cleaner and safer the world might be if we could replace all fossil fuels with biogas and other forms of renewable clean energy that you'll read about later. Together with planting more forests and protecting whales that help oceans absorb extra carbon dioxide, we could SAVE THE WORLD and carry on pooping forever!

**In a nutshell . . . why "poop gas" can be great news for the planet:**

💩 It is a renewable source of energy, which means that it will not run out, as long as people and animals keep pooping.

💩 Although carbon dioxide is released when biogas is burned, it originally came from plants that once absorbed carbon dioxide. So the only extra carbon dioxide emitted is from machinery used in the process.

💩 It uses up waste materials without the need for expensive, dangerous, and environmentally damaging mining.

SAVE OUR PLANET!

So, what is your verdict now . . . POOP–friend, foe, or superhero?

CHAPTER 5

# POOP IN ACTION

## ENERGY FROM BEHIND

Biogas made from sewage hasn't saved the world yet but it's certainly lighting it up. It fuels electric generators to make electricity for homes and streets, and power stations to supply small towns. Around the world, biogas electricity is already powering millions of homes. One day, poop could be powering entire cities and railroads.

## Switching on our behinds

The daily poop from about 100,000 people can now generate electricity for 3,000–5,000 LED energy-saving light bulbs. If this could be improved and scaled up to use all human and animal waste, what a difference that could make to the world.

## Hot and steamy

One of the biggest heating systems to use raw sewage is in Norway. Just by flushing their toilets, people heat their homes and offices. Machines at a tunnel in Oslo suck heat from the sewers and send it to a network of pipes that supply thousands of radiators and hot water pipes in the city. That's 100 poo-cent clean energy!

## Horsepower

The Helsinki International Horse Show in Finland has been powered by 110 tons of horse manure. It was used to power the four day show with 150 megawatts of electricity. That's enough to power about 30,000 homes for an hour.

## Mule poop lights up a mountain

Kedarnath in North India has about 7,000 mules for carrying pilgrims to mountain shrines. Lots of mule dung once washed into the river but now it's collected to generate electricity. A single power plant can turn 2,755 pounds of dung (the weight of three whole mules) into 50kW of electricity each day for powering 25 houses, as well as streetlights. How's that for LIGHT donkey work?

**UGGGHHH!**

## Every little helps

A cow can make about 110 pounds of dung in a day (that's heavier than most 12-year-olds, but maybe a bit smellier!). That's enough to power three 100-watt light bulbs for 10 hours.

# Zoo poop

Some zoos busily turn their endless supply of dung into power. After all, poop is the one substance zoos have in mega-piles.

In 2017, Detroit Zoo became the first in the US to convert animal waste to clean energy. The manure as well as food waste goes straight into a biodigester. Electricity from all that biogas powers the zoo's animal hospital. Leftover solids make superb compost for the zoo's gardens. More zoos are now developing ways to recycle their poop supplies and stop waste going to waste.

Canada's Toronto Zoo also has plenty of dung donors. Vishnu, the one-horned rhino, can produce enough dung in a year to power a home for 72 days. By running its biogas electricity plant, the zoo uses 33,000 tons of manure and food waste. That doesn't just provide much of the zoo's electricity (equivalent to powering 500 homes), it will cut its $CO_2$ emissions by 11,000 tons.

## A walk in the park

In some town parks around the world, dog owners bag up their pets' poop for firing up streetlights. All you have to do is pop your dog's waste into a special box in the park. This mini digester just needs a quick stir with a hand crank. As methane is released, it gets piped through the ground to a streetlamp where a flame lights up the area. Dogs will probably like lampposts even more now.

## Little POOch

Since you've been reading this book, thousands of tons of dog poop have plopped onto Earth. Think how much energy all that dog waste could generate when a dog's average daily deposit is enough to power an electric fan for two hours! The problem is how to scoop all that poop.

PICK UP AFTER YOUR DOG!

Which is the best breed of dog for providing lamplight? Poodles, of course!

# In the back of beyond

Poop can come to the rescue of people living without any electricity in very remote areas. They don't need mules, elephants, rhinos, dogs, horses, or cows. How about guinea pigs? Don't worry ... the little rodents aren't made to run all day in hamster wheels to turn the electric turbines. All they have to do is eat, rest, and poop.

Remote villages in Peru in South America keep almost a thousand guinea pigs in enclosures. The rodents are farmed for their droppings—small, dry pellets that are fed into biodigesters. Add water, stir, and wait. The result is methane and rich liquid fertilizer. One village uses 3.3 tons of guinea pig droppings each month to power light bulbs, stoves, and TVs. Selling the liquid fertilizer makes the village extra cash, too.

That's good news for poor rural communities who can use poop power to improve their lives. You may be surprised at how others are using their own poop to earn a few little extras ...
coming next.

# Pay as you go

Have you heard the one about the toilet that pays you to poop? It's no joke—it's TRUE! "Spending a penny" was always a term for going to the bathroom because that's what it used to cost to use a public toilet. But now a public toilet in South Korea can pay you back.

The BeeVi toilet uses a vacuum pump instead of water to suck poop into a digester tank, where bacteria turn it into methane. The gas then provides energy and hot water for a university. Students using the toilet earn a type of digital currency, which can be used to pay for coffee or buy noodles, fruit, and books. Maybe poop for profit isn't such a bad idea...

An average person's daily poop could make 13 gallons of methane gas, according to a professor at the university. That can generate electricity or provide fuel to drive a car.

**So, students ... top marks for your brain power and poop power!**

WELCOME

# CHAPTER 6

# POOPTASTIC NEWS

## MAJOR MOVEMENTS IN SCIENCE

A chief contributor to greenhouse emissions is the car. Since 2010 there have been over one billion cars on the world's roads. Together with all the trucks and semi-trailers adding to their fumes, transport causes about one-fifth of all the world's carbon dioxide emissions.

No wonder many world leaders and car makers are looking to poop for a sweet-smelling answer.

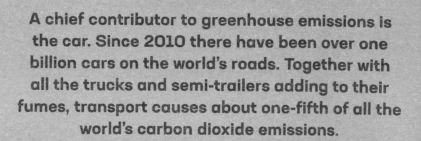

# Poop on wheels

The USA is powering-up all sorts of heavy vehicles from biogas fuel. One project uses human sewage to drive a city's working fleet of vehicles. Grand Junction in Colorado fuels garbage trucks, street sweepers, dump trucks and buses with biofuel. If more cities continue to follow, what a difference that could make to overall carbon emissions.

## Bio buses

Public transport is full of poop possibilities! Britain's first "poop bus" running on biogas fuel from human sewage and household waste went into service in Bristol in 2015. The local sewage treatment works was the first and largest to produce upgraded methane-rich biogas. One tankful powers the bus for 185 miles.

## Sweden and Norway

The first international bus to run on liquid biogas began operating between Stockholm and Oslo in 2021. Technology has developed so biogas can be cooled to minus 265 °F so that it becomes liquid and more energy-dense. This makes it possible to fuel heavy transport for longer distances by land and sea. Biogas is now really going places. Half of Europe's heavy-duty gas-fueled transport could be powered by biogas in 2025—poop power is certainly on the move like never before.

## The fastest toilet on the road

If whizzing along the open road while sitting on a toilet is your preferred way to travel, you might want to buy the Toilet Bike Neo from Japan. Yes, it's a poop-powered motorcycle! Although the rider sits on a toilet seat, you might be relieved to know the motorbike isn't really a working toilet. The manufacturer just wanted to make the point that their eco-friendly, poop-powered motorcycle runs on biogas at your convenience. When it first appeared, it certainly made a splash!

The Spanish car maker Seat is developing biogas cars where the main ingredient is pig dung. In a country with 50 million pigs, there's plenty of raw material to use. So far, the biogas cars emit 25 percent less carbon dioxide than gasoline cars and far fewer polluting particles. One problem is the extra cost of these cars and a lack of refueling stations. But these should improve—and maybe the contribution of pigs to cleaner travel will keep growing. That's the HAM-bition!

## Moving on

Since a Volkswagen Beetle car was powered by biogas in 2010 and called "The Dung Beetle," cars with poop behind them have been catching on. It was claimed then that the sewage from 70 UK homes was enough to power the VW Dung Beetle for 10,000 miles. Australia took things further and headlines appeared, such as:

NEWS

First Human Waste Powered Car Kicks Up A Stink

A Mitsubishi i-MiEV was powered by electricity generated from the waste of about 300,000 flushing Brisbane homes. Then in 2021 came The Hyundai Kona electric SUV. This "new improved" electric car

- uses 40,000 gallons of Australian sewage to charge its battery to full

- saves around $1,700 in gasoline every year

- has a 280-mile range on a single charge and with zero emissions.

- Or, if you're not going far, one person's output could power the car for a third of a mile. You might need to "pay a visit" to get you home again!

# On the right track?

Going by train is usually a cleaner way to travel because railways no longer pollute the air like the time of steam trains. After all, electric trains produce no belching smoke. However, some of the world's railways use electricity made by burning fossil fuels.

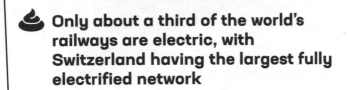

## DID YOU KNOW?

💩 Only about a third of the world's railways are electric, with Switzerland having the largest fully electrified network

💩 As diesel trains run on fossil fuel, they emit carbon dioxide

💩 About 29% of the UK's trains use diesel and the plan is to phase them out by 2040

So what can be used instead?
Yes, you've guessed it!

New lightweight trains powered by sewage are on the way. Britain is developing railcars that convert poop biogas into electricity to charge its batteries. The railcar, about 66 feet long and with a top speed of 50 miles per hour can carry up to 120 passengers. These super-green mini-trains are planned to replace diesel trains on branch lines that aren't electrified. Once more, the future is poop.

## The sky's the limit

Aircraft are known to have a big impact on the environment. Flying is often blamed for producing too much greenhouse gas. Even so, it only contributes about 2.5 percent of all carbon dioxide emissions. Aircraft engineers are no longer sitting on the job by just thinking about cutting pollution from planes. They're rolling up their sleeves and getting to grips with poop.

The Japanese airline All Nippon Airways is cleaning up its fuel by using rabbit poop. Chemicals in the droppings can be used in developing a cleaner type of aviation fuel. Maybe the airline will now be called Nippon HARE-WAYS.

Scientists have also developed a new chemical way to turn sewage into paraffin, as an ingredient of jet fuel. The new fuel blend could reduce airline emissions to almost zero. With over 21 billion gallons of jet fuel used a year in the United States alone (probably doubling by 2050), "poop paraffin" could really start to takeoff.

So where do you stand on POOP now (hopefully not in bare feet)—friend, foe, or superhero?

# CHAPTER 7

# ANOTHER WEE SOLUTION

## THE FUTURE IS GOLDEN

It isn't just poop with locked-in power. Another bodily waste can also come gushing to our rescue. The hidden powers of our liquid waste have long been put to use. Although 95% of our urine is water, there are also useful chemicals in the mix. The nitrogen and hydrogen in stale urine can make ammonia, which is a powerful cleaning agent.

Some Ancient Romans liked to whiten their teeth with a strong mouthwash. No, it wasn't minty fresh—just yucky yellow. It was undiluted human or animal urine. Not only that, but Roman street corners also often had pots for anyone to pee into. The contents went off to a laundry called a fullonica. Workers would pour all the urine into tubs of dirty clothes, then jump inside with bare feet and stomp away. The result was clean clothes, wrinkly feet, and an interesting lingering fragrance.

GROSS ALERT! Don't read the next bit if you're feeling delicate ...

Ingredients of Urine
0.05% Ammonia
0.18% Sulphate
0.12% Phosphate
0.6% Chloride
0.01% Magnesium
0.015% Calcium
0.6% Potassium
0.1% Sodium
0.1% Creatinine
0.03% Uric acid
2% Urea
95% Water

MY MOUTHWASH RECIPEE FOR A DAZZLING ROMAN SMILE!

## Peeing gold

People always wondered about urine's golden color. Would you believe, back in 1669, a German scientist named Hennig Brand boiled up a vat of urine in the hope of making gold. He ended up with a paste that he heated into a waxy substance that glowed in the dark. He had discovered phosphorus—which was later used to make matchheads. It was useful but dangerous.

## Urine danger

In 1862, an American scientist wrote a handy recipe for making gunpowder involving a manure heap. "Water every week with the richest kinds of liquid manure, such as urine, dung-water, water of privies, cess-pools, and drains. The mixture is stirred every week and, after several months, no more pee is added." For health and safety reasons, we can't tell you what to do next, but don't strike a match!

# Urine for a surprise

With over eight billion people on our planet, something like three billion gallons of human urine is produced each day. That's getting on for 5,000 Olympic-sized swimming pools full—not that you'd want to swim in them! That could be enough to keep Niagara Falls going for up to an hour. In other words, it's masses of liquid going to waste.

So, with all that urine about, there's a lot of urea, too. That's a substance dissolved in the urine of mammals, formed by the breaking down of proteins in the body. Urea contains carbon, nitrogen, and oxygen, and can be used in fertilizers, plastics, and medicines. But scientists are turning it into energy.

CLEAN UREA-POWERED CARS, HOMES, AND ELECTRICAL DEVICES ARE ALREADY ON THE WAY.

# Pee-lectricity

In 2012, four schoolgirls made a small, urine-powered generator—and a big impression—at a Nigerian science fair. They wanted to show how a remote home could use urine to make electricity.

**What they did . . .**

• Put some urine into an electrical cell, which separated out hydrogen. An electrical cell is a small container that creates chemical and electrical reactions.

• Put the hydrogen through a filter to purify it, then stored it in a gas cylinder.

• Ran an electric generator, burning the hydrogen gas to make electricity but no greenhouse gas.

## DID YOU KNOW?

Hydrogen is a colorless and odorless gas that's lighter than air. Mixed with oxygen it makes water, so we have lots of hydrogen in our bodies and in our urine. When hydrogen is released from water as a gas, it catches fire easily.

# Batter-wee power

Urine's mix of minerals and bacteria can also generate power in a special battery. A small amount of urine soaks a fine mesh of fibers, then microbes can feed on the bacteria. Hey presto—this releases energy from a stack of "fuel cells" and provides enough electricity to power light bulbs or phones. Scientists hope to run whole houses and streets with this technology. The other good news is the urine is cleaned up in the process, so the only leftovers are clean water and solids that make a great crop fertilizer.

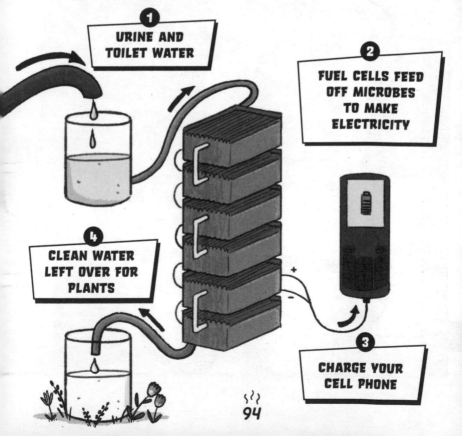

**1** URINE AND TOILET WATER

**2** FUEL CELLS FEED OFF MICROBES TO MAKE ELECTRICITY

**4** CLEAN WATER LEFT OVER FOR PLANTS

**3** CHARGE YOUR CELL PHONE

## Light relief

Some schools in remote parts of Africa where electricity is unreliable or non-existent have been making their own power. How? Yes, by wiring up their toilet blocks to harness all that pee power. Urine trickles into stacks of fuel cells and enough electricity is made to power lights and charge cell phones. With around one-seventh of the world's population lacking access to basic electricity, pee power isn't such a potty idea!

## The future looks apPEEling

Imagine you're on a mission in the jungle. You must send an urgent message, but your phone is dead. How do you charge it fast? Soldiers working in remote areas have the answer. Army scientists have developed what they call "aluminum nanopowder" that instantly turns urine into hydrogen, which quickly powers-up fuel cells for clean electric energy.

Just over two pounds of powder can make 220 kilowatts in just three minutes. That's more than enough to charge an electric vehicle for a few hours over many miles. As this technology improves, maybe we could see electric cars being charged from urine—but don't expect to see fuel stations filling up your tank with it!

## Whatever next?

Could pee power join forces with poop power to be the energy force of the future? Will they both bring heat and light to the billion people around the world who don't have access to electricity? But that's not all. Both can produce hydrogen. If you dream of the future powered by super-clean "green hydrogen," just see what's coming next...

PEE—friend, foe, or superhero?

CHAPTER 8

# SITTING ON A TIME BOMB

## THE FIZZING FUTURE OF POOP POWER

Turning sewage into clean hydrogen fuel to replace all fossil fuel may seem too good to be true but now the science is on the move. Hydrogen is now used in a range of vehicles—with electric power generated from fuel cells and as fuel in combustion engines. Engineers are now working on storing solid hydrogen in car fuel tanks. This would allow vehicles to store more hydrogen and travel farther before needing to refuel.

# HYDROGEN CHECK LIST

☑ found everywhere on Earth

☑ flammable as a gas, solid, or liquid

☑ as fuel it leaves no pollution—just water

☑ poop and pee are renewable sources of hydrogen

☑ technology is advancing to make hydrogen fuel cheaper, more efficient, and manageable

☑ Liquid hydrogen forms under high pressure and very low temperatures. Stored this way, hydrogen takes up less space than its normal gas form. Liquid hydrogen has long been used as rocket fuel—so get ready for takeoff ...

## How it works

Liquid hydrogen burns when it is mixed with oxygen gas and ignited. As the fuel burns, it shoots out hot gas (steam) which thrusts the rocket upward or forward. This action is called jet propulsion. Rockets must travel at over 25,000 miles per hour to get into space. That's about 7.5 miles per second. The engine combustion chamber can reach 6,000 °F. Hot stuff!

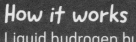

**DID YOU KNOW?**

**The first rockets were invented in 10th century China, by attaching gunpowder to arrows. It wasn't until the 1940s that rocket science really began to take off. Quick to aim for the stars, China has now launched more space rockets than any country.**

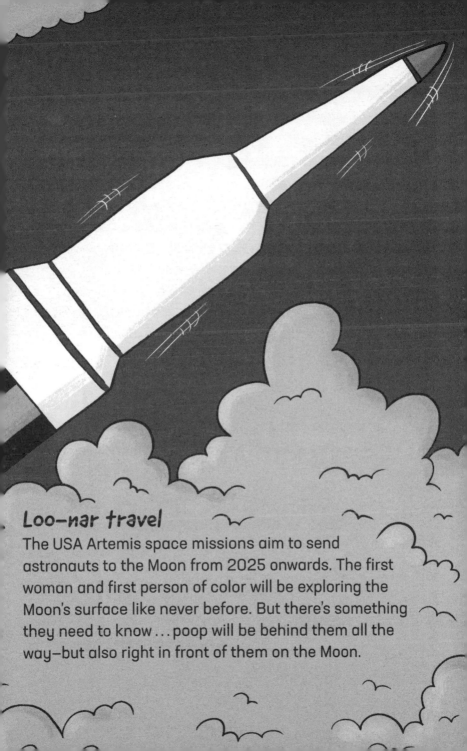

## Loo-nar travel

The USA Artemis space missions aim to send astronauts to the Moon from 2025 onwards. The first woman and first person of color will be exploring the Moon's surface like never before. But there's something they need to know... poop will be behind them all the way—but also right in front of them on the Moon.

## Poop in space

NASA is researching ways of turning astronaut poop into biogas fuel up in space. They think they can produce enough rocket fuel on a trip to fly from the Moon back to Earth. Carrying less fuel but making it on the way would make rockets of the future far more efficient.

Space scientists are also developing a fuel cell that can extract electricity from poop onboard a spacecraft. On a two-year trip to Mars, a crew of six would produce tons of poop which could make a lot of power. When will this happen? Watch this SPACE.

# Endless poop on the Moon

If you ever decide to go to the Moon, be careful where you tread. Astronauts have left plenty of waste behind, including bags of poop. It will probably never rot away as there are no bacteria there to clear it up. Even so, some scientists are keen to go back to peep at the poop to see if the bacteria that were already inside have survived ... or maybe escaped!

## UFOs (Unidentified Fiery Objects)

In case you were wondering ... astronauts at the International Space Station poop into a little toilet hole, where a vacuum pump sucks their excrement away. It gets stored in containers before being ejected into space, where it burns up as it whizzes to Earth. Yes, that means some of the shooting stars we might see are actually astronaut poop burning up in the atmosphere. And as for astronauts' urine—none of it goes to waste. It all gets cleaned up and made into drinking water again. Pee-licious.

## 3...2...1...we have pants off!

In case you were still wondering...smelly pants in
space can also be put to good use. Russian scientists
came up with a method of using bacteria to digest
astronauts' used cotton and paper underwear. Apart
from making unwanted yucky underpants rot away, the
bacteria make biogas, which could be used to help fuel
the spacecraft. You may not think it's rocket science,
but one day we might be over the moon thanks to
grubby underpants.

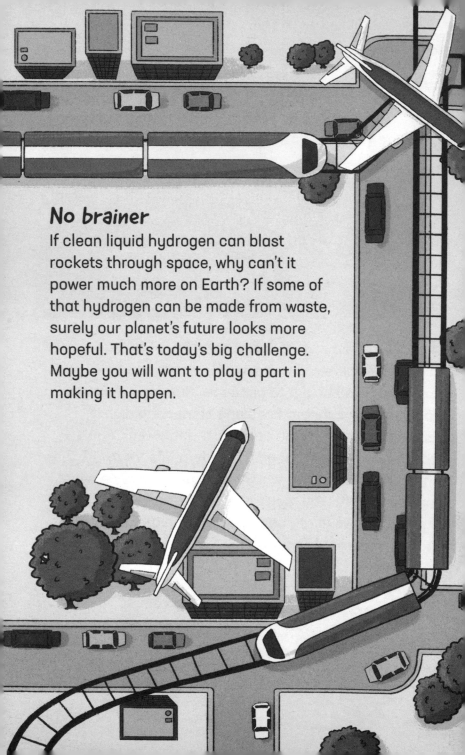

## No brainer

If clean liquid hydrogen can blast rockets through space, why can't it power much more on Earth? If some of that hydrogen can be made from waste, surely our planet's future looks more hopeful. That's today's big challenge. Maybe you will want to play a part in making it happen.

## Tomorrow's world

Fuel made from bodily waste has much to offer, despite some problems. Expense and availability of hydrogen needs to improve. When liquid hydrogen warms, it evaporates, which means a car left for days in the sun could lose fuel. Even so, there are clear signs that clean vehicles fueled by hydrogen are the future of pollution-free travel. Hydrogen trains are beginning to whiz down the tracks, and some aircraft are already fueled by liquid hydrogen—although the cost is still much higher than flying with standard jet fuel. If we choose to fly only with airlines that use "green fuel," perhaps we can help to make a difference. That seems like PLANE common sense!

So, what is your verdict now . . . POOP—friend, foe, or superhero?

# Three cheers for other cool fuels

**Apart from the recent growth in poop power and biomass energy, other renewable fuels are on the rise, too. They will eventually take over from fossil fuels to make electricity and drastically cut greenhouse gas emissions.**

## Feeling windy

All around the world huge wind turbines are whirring to make plenty of clean electricity. Vast wind farms with many turbines are lighting and heating millions of homes. The Gansu Wind Farm in China is the largest in the world, aiming for 7,000 wind turbines. That's enough to power 15 million homes! But even one single offshore wind turbine out at sea can power well over 3,000 homes. It's a shame we can't work out a way to harness the power of our personal wind emissions!

The most well-known view of wind turbines are these tall towers with white blades. But engineers are also looking into alternative designs that are more efficient, including bladeless turbines that wobble in the wind.

BLADELESS TURBINE

## Water power

Running water has driven machines for hundreds of years. When it drives turbines, water generates super-clean electricity. Building dams that hold back great reservoirs, then releasing jets of water down pipes to drive turbines is already generating much of the world's electricity. Over half the world's renewable energy is currently generated by hydroelectric power. The world's largest hydroelectric dam is the Three Gorges Dam in China, which can generate electricity for about 17 million homes. That's mega-power!

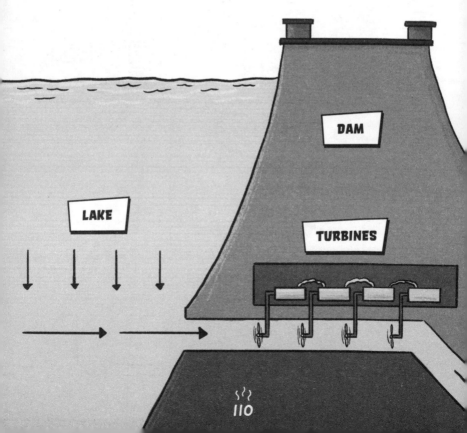

## Sunshine good times

Large panels full of solar cells can convert sunlight directly into electricity. Solar cells have no moving parts and need no fuel. They just have to be kept clean to keep them working well. Solar farms packed with rows of big solar panels can generate clean electricity for millions of homes. Smaller solar cells are being used more in buildings, road signs, bus stops, and even on backpacks for charging up phones and tablets.

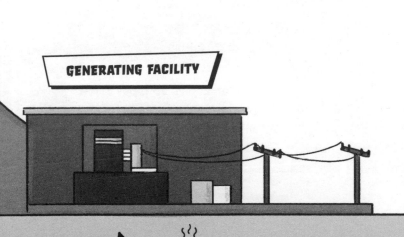

**GENERATING FACILITY**

# Geothermal energy

If you drill down far enough beneath your feet, you will reach very hot rock. Earth's inner heat can give us clean energy called geothermal power ("geo" means earth and "thermal" means heat). In Iceland, where hot rocks are close to the surface, homes are heated with underground energy.

COOLING TOWER

GENERATOR

TURBINE

STEAM

COLD WATER

HOT WATER

Hot water comes up pipes from below ground into radiators. When it's cool again, the water pumps back below ground to be reheated.

In fact, Iceland generates the cleanest electricity per person in the world. Nearly 100% of Iceland's energy comes from renewable sources: 72% from hydropower and 28% from geothermal energy.

# What's your verdict?

**Although "green fuels" have a vital future, they each currently have a few drawbacks:**

 Wind—it's not always windy

 Solar—it's not always sunny (like at night!)

 Hydroelectric power needs plenty of water and rainfall. Building dams and reservoirs is expensive and can harm the local environment

 Geothermal isn't suitable where the hot rock is too deep inside Earth

 But for poop power none of the above problems apply and there's a never-ending supply! By 2030, all biomass is expected to be the biggest source of renewable energy in the world (for heating and electricity).

## To sum up . . .

Climate change is with us, and it won't go away . . . yet.
People are responsible for much of it—particularly in
richer countries. Global warming is a threat to us all
and many countries are trying to do something about it.
There are great opportunities and solutions—poop
is one of them. How we recycle all our waste is crucial
to the future of our planet. Are you ready for
the challenge?

We can all take care of our environment and do little things to cut down the amount of $CO_2$ we each release into the air. The amount you release from your own energy needs is known as your carbon footprint. Apart from demanding higher standards from water companies to recycle our sewage in better ways, each of us can take a few steps to make a difference. Coming up next are just a few...

## SAVE ENERGY

- Turn off lights, TVs, and other devices, when not needed
- Fill dishwashers, washing machines, and driers rather than using them half-empty
- Only put the amount of water you need in the kettle
- Use low energy light bulbs.

# How you can ...

## SAVE WATER

- Take shorter showers
- Turn off the tap while brushing your teeth to avoid letting the water run
- Collect rainwater to water your plants.

## GROW PLANTS

- Ask your school to plant some $CO_2$-absorbing plants, shrubs, and trees, or plant some yourself
- Growing vegetables and making compost from kitchen waste is good fun and worth trying
- Ask your family to buy from local growers to cut $CO_2$ from transport.

## RECYCLE

- Use the right recycling bin for glass, paper, cans, plastic, and clothes
- Instead of plastic bags, use any bag that can be used lots of times
- Use a drinks bottle that can be refilled, instead of throwaway bottles.

# ...help save the world

## CHOOSE WELL

- Eating seasonal food (with reduced packaging) cuts down airmiles
- Eating less meat reduces the need for intensive livestock farming, which consumes vast amounts of grain and produces methane
- Walking and cycling are better for you and the planet, rather than traveling by car
- Wear an extra sweater or blanket instead of turning up the heat.

## Sewage sense

Everyone can help sewage companies recycle our toilet waste if we only flush the **3 Ps—poop, pee, and paper** (toilet tissue only). Anything else causes blockages or stops bacteria breaking down the sludge. That means no wet wipes, cotton wool, cotton buds, food waste, or general rubbish down the toilet. And only pour water down the sink. Giant fatbergs in sewers cause a lot of damage. These are gross, solid masses that build up from flushed non-biodegradable solids and "FOG"—fat, oil, and grease.

## Learn more

This book has helped you understand a little about why it's important to find greener ways of powering our planet.

Use your local library to find out more, and to discover what else you can do to protect the wonderful world we call home.

# Flush-friendly advice

**TOILET PAPER ONLY**

## The big debate—over

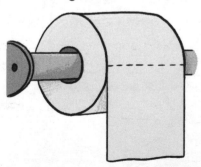

EVERYTHING ELSE (even if labeled flushable)

or under?

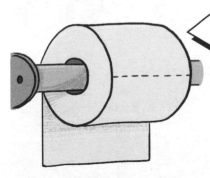

Despite the wonders of modern toilet paper, it still causes arguments in some families!

## Saving the world

The future of our planet depends on all of us. Many countries are already working to save energy and increase renewable energy. Climate change will remain a serious challenge so tackling carbon emissions and recycling waste may take decades. Maybe world leaders will get behind poop power, sit down together, and push for action!

# Flushing away the doom

Although Earth will be at risk of overheating for years ahead, there is still time to act. Yet the question remains—can poop save the world?

If we all want it to, poop can make a very big try. Although it can't save the world on its own, poop has great poo-tential for cutting carbon emissions. So, will the world vote for poop to be the new superpower? As far as many of us are concerned, the motion is already passed!

# POO WANTS TO BE A MILLIONAIRE?

**Test your knowledge on all things poopy. Warning—only the first three questions have been covered in the book!**

## Q1. What is fossilized poop called?

- [ ] a) Coprolite
- [ ] b) Dinolite
- [ ] c) Poopalite

## Q2. What was the nickname for a car run on poop biogas?

- [ ] a) Winnie the Poo
- [ ] b) VW Dung Beetle
- [ ] c) Excreta Four-Seater

## Q3. Why is whale poop important to ocean ecosystems?

- [ ] a) It provides nutrients to surface organisms
- [ ] b) It makes the seabed soft for deep water shellfish
- [ ] c) It keeps away dangerous sharks

## Q4. Why do guinea pigs eat their droppings?

- [ ] a) To annoy their parents
- [ ] b) It tastes like toffee
- [ ] c) To digest extra vitamins

## Q5. What is the HAWC Mk1?

- [ ] a) A car that runs on concentrated urine (Human Auto Widdle Concentrate)
- [ ] b) A plane fueled by sewage hydrogen (Hydrogen Aircraft Waste Charger)
- [ ] c) The fastest motorized toilet at over 70 mph (Highly Advanced Water Closet)

## Q6. In World War II, why did the British make explosives to look like camel dung?

- [ ] a) Italian soldiers marching in the desert would always kick dung out of their way
- [ ] b) German tank drivers thought it was good luck to drive over camel dung
- [ ] c) Japanese troops used camel dung as fuel on their campfires

## Q7. What's unusual about the way hippos poop?

- [ ] a) They flap their tail and spatter poop in all directions
- [ ] b) They dig a hole then roll in it
- [ ] c) They stand on two legs

## Q8. Why do baby elephants eat their mothers' droppings?

- [ ] a) To please their fathers
- [ ] b) To keep away predators
- [ ] c) To improve their digestive system with useful gut flora

## Q9. What is the old name for a ship toilet?

- [ ] a) The head
- [ ] b) The poop deck
- [ ] c) The Long John

## Q10. Which of these is a real product you can buy?

- [ ] a) Fox faeces soap
- [ ] b) Dormouse droppings candy
- [ ] c) Panda poop tea

Answers: 1a, 2b, 3a, 4c, 5c, 6b, 7a, 8c, 9a, 10c